NATURAL RELIGION

IN

INDIA.

T0345988

NATURAL RELIGION

IN

INDIA

THE REDE LECTURE
DELIVERED IN THE SENATE-HOUSE
ON JUNE 17, 1891.

BY

Sɪʀ ALFRED LYALL, K.C.B., K.C.I.E.

CAMBRIDGE:
AT THE UNIVERSITY PRESS.

1891

CAMBRIDGE
UNIVERSITY PRESS

University Printing House, Cambridge CB2 8BS, United Kingdom

Published in the United States of America by Cambridge University Press, New York

Cambridge University Press is part of the University of Cambridge.

It furthers the University's mission by disseminating knowledge in the pursuit of education, learning and research at the highest international levels of excellence.

www.cambridge.org
Information on this title: www.cambridge.org/9781107623569

© Cambridge University Press 1891

First published 1891
First paperback edition 2014

A catalogue record for this publication is available from the British Library

ISBN 978-1-107-62356-9 Paperback

NATURAL RELIGION IN INDIA.

I SHALL not endeavour to give, in this single
lecture, any general description of Indian Religions. Nor do I propose to make any appre-
ciable addition to the vast heap of facts and
anecdotes, fables and folklore, that have been
already collected in support of different theories
regarding the origin of myth, ritual, primitive
worships, and rudimentary belief. My present
purpose is to draw attention, briefly, to the
particular importance of India as a field of
observation and research in identifying and
tracing through connected stages the growth and
filiation of some of the principal ideas that
undoubtedly lie at the roots of Natural Religion.

When I speak of Religion in India, I mean, for the purpose of this Lecture, Hinduism. And if I were asked for a definition of Hinduism, I could give no precise answer; I could not define it concisely by giving its central doctrines and its essential articles of faith; as I might do in describing one of the great historical Religions. For the word Hindu is not exclusively a religious denomination ; it denotes also a country, and to a certain degree a race. When we speak of a Christian, a Mahomedan, or a Buddhist, we mean a particular religious community, in the widest sense, without distinction of race or place. When we talk of a Russian or a Persian, we indicate country or parentage without distinction of creed. But when a man tells me that he is a Hindu, I know that he means all three things together—Religion, Parentage, and Country. I can be almost sure that he is an inhabitant of India, I know that he is an Indian by birth and descent; and as to his religion, the word Hindu, though it is rather indefinite, undoubtedly places him within one of the many groups or castes that follow the ordinances and worship the gods who are recognized by the Brahmans.

I would ask you to remark that we have here at once, at the first word, a significant indication of the peculiar character and composition of Hinduism. This triple meaning or connotation of the term Hindu shews the complexity of its origin, shews how Hinduism is twisted deep among the roots of Indian society, how it is a matter of birthright and inheritance; signifies that it means a civil community, quite as much as a religious association—that a man does not become a Hindu, but is born into Hinduism.

Let me illustrate this view of Hinduism, as different in type, origin, and constitution from the other great Religions, by pointing to its position on what I may call a Religious Map of the World—I suppose that in fact the geographical areas occupied by the chief religions have often been mapped out. We may put aside Africa as wholly barbarous and benighted, except where its edges have been touched by light from Asia. Then such a map, supposing that it gave only the broad outlines and divisions, would exhibit all Europe and America overspread by Christianity, and in Asia it would shew that the three grand Historic Faiths or Creeds—Christianity, Islam, and Buddhism,—have made a nominal partition of the whole Continent, with the notable exception of one country. It would be seen that in all the three Continents there is one, and only one, country of the first magnitude, only one large population of settled civilization, that is not annexed to, or at least claimed by, one or another of these three Spiritual empires; and that people are the Hindus. If we mark off roughly the spheres of religion in Asia, we shall find that Western and Central Asia, from the Red Sea and the Mediterranean to the borders of India and the Chinese empire, is, speaking broadly, Mahomedan. On the other

side, in Eastern and North-Eastern Asia, throughout China, in Japan, Burmah, and Siam, the established Church, the Faith that is incontestably
predominant though not exclusively accepted,
is Buddhist. So that while the West and centre
of Asia are worshippers of one God, in the whole
of Eastern Asia Buddhism, which acknowledges
no supreme personal deity, still holds the chief
place, and maintains a kind of high catholic
dominion. The people who stand between
but stand apart from both monotheism and
Buddhism, are the Hindus; they are the sole
surviving representatives of a great polytheistic
system. We have in India a people that have
been incessantly conquered politically, but never
overpowered or subdued spiritually, that have
expelled Buddhism, successfully resisted Islam,
and have been very little affected even by
Christianity. Hinduism has preserved its inde-
pendence between two powerful and imposing
religious sovereignties—between Islam the Faith
militant, and Buddhism the Faith contemplative,

the religion of Action and the religion of
Thought. The 200 millions of Hindus consti-
tute the only considerable section of more or less
civilized humanity that does not at this moment
acquiesce in the religious authority of Buddha,
of Mahomet, or of some Christian Church.

Now it must always be remembered that the
Indians are not a rude and unintelligent folk
upon whom great intellectual movements take
little hold. On the contrary, they are the most
subtle minded and profoundly devout people in
Asia. And so far am I from regarding Hinduism as unconnected with the deeper currents
of spiritual ideas, that I take India to be one of
the religious watersheds of the world. I mean
that as from some high ridge or plateau the
rivers rise and run down into distant lands,
so from India there has been a large outflow
of religious ideas over Asia. It has of course
been the fountain head of Buddhism, which
has flooded, as I have said, all Eastern Asia;
while I believe that the influence of Indian

theosophy spread at the beginning of the Christian era as far West as Alexandria. I am
told that it profoundly affected the ancient
religion of Persia; and it is plainly traceable
later in the mysticism of the Persian Sufis.
But while the religious thought of India has
thus radiated out East and West across the
Asiatic Continent, I doubt whether Hinduism,
the immemorial religion of the Indian people,
has in all these ages assimilated a single important or prolific idea from outside India. The
current of ideas is not always above ground, it
often subsides and reappears; but it seems to
me to have flowed steadily out of India; until
its natural course was disturbed by the violent
irruption of Islam. It is in this manner that
Hinduism may be said to represent high religious
ground that has been for ages a dividing line
between the great religious systems that have
overspread the countries on either side of it. Its
characteristic is the entire absence of system; it
has never been under the political control or regu-

lation of a State; it has never been organized ecclesiastically. For, in the first place, the long dominion in India of foreigners, aliens in race and religion, seems to me not only to have arrested the intellectual development of Hinduism during the last eight hundred years, but also to have kept it in a dislocated and inorganic condition. And secondly the Hindu priesthood, though powerful, has never been able to bring within specific limits the wandering beliefs of an intensely superstitious people. The Brahmans exercise immense authority, yet they have never obtained any effective mastery over the incessant movements and changes of belief and ritual in Hinduism. The result has been that there prevails, and has always prevailed, a great incoherence and diversity in the divine affairs of India; there has been a loose and luxuriant growth of religious fancies and usages; and the religion has become a conglomerate of rude worship and high liturgies, of superstitions and philosophies, belonging to very different phases of society and mental culture. I doubt whether there is anything like it in any other part of the world. And I regard Hinduism as a survival from those early ages when in the midst of a highly organized civil society Religion was still in a state of confusion ; before the rise and establishment of the great historic Churches and Creeds which have since made a partition of the old world, from Ireland Eastward to the Indus. From looking closely at India as it is we can best form a notion of ancient polytheism, not such as that which in Europe we have for centuries called paganism because it lingered longest in the rural districts, but polytheism before its decline and fall, when it was the religion of the civilized world under the Roman empire. Such is Hinduism as we still see it flourishing in India ; and for the purposes of this lecture I propose to call it Natural Religion.

Now I do not of course use the term Natural Religion in the sense given to it by Bishop

Butler, when he said that Christianity was a republication of Natural Religion. He meant, I think, religion according to right reason, framed upon the principle of accepting the course and constitution of Nature as an index of the Divine Will. The meaning that I wish to convey is of Religion in what Hobbes would call a State of Nature, moulded only by circumstances and feelings, and founded upon analogies drawn sometimes with ignorant simplicity, sometimes with great subtlety, from the operation of natural agencies and phenomena. The presence, the doings, and the character of numerous superhuman beings are thus directly inferred from what actually happens to men in the world around them ; and a mysterious kind of design is perceived in every uncommon motion, or shape, or sensation. What is it that evidently suggests the intentions and sets the model of divinity thus realized ? Nothing but capricious and freely acting Nature; the religious feeling works by taking impressions or reflections, sometimes rough and grotesque, sometimes refined and artistic, from all that men hear and feel and see. This is what I desire to call Natural Religion, because it has grown up in this manner spontaneously out of the free play of man's fears and hopes, and his guesses at the truth of this unintelligible world. I mean a religion that has not yet acquired a distinctive form and a settled base, but is constantly springing up and reproducing itself under different shapes, in diverse species ; and throwing out varieties of rite and worship according to the changing needs and conditions of the people. I have no doubt whatever that in many uncivilized countries something of this kind is always going on. But I believe that in no modern country has Natural Religion been as long undisturbed, or has reached anything like the height or expansion that it has attained in India. My point is that Hinduism can be seen growing, that one can discern the earliest notions, rude and vague, among the primitive jungle tribes, that one can see the same ideas and practices upon a higher level, in more distinct and reasonable shape, among the settled classes; and that one can follow them upwards until they merge into allegory, mysticism, or abstract philosophical conceptions. I think that it is possible to trace in India, less obscurely than elsewhere, the development of natural into supernatural beliefs. I do not pretend that India contains any very rare or unusual kinds of ritual or worship ; for nothing is more remarkable than the persistent similarity of such ideas and practices among primitive folk. What makes India so valuable as a field of observation, is that the various forms and species lie close together in one country at the same time, so that their differences and affinities can be compared. In short, I believe that India, from its position in the world, from its past history, from its present state, and because it is an antique society thoroughly accessible to modern research, presents an almost unique opportunity for the comprehensive study of the History of Natural Religion.

The time at my disposal to-day only allows me to illustrate this position by reference to a few of the most universal and prolific among primary religious beliefs. Let me take the theory that Dreams and Ghosts are the sources of the earliest superstitions—it is a theory much in vogue at the present time, though it is by no means a modern discovery. Now the evidence that can be collected and brought to bear from India on this theory is abundant and exceedingly impressive, because it brings out perceptible links and gradations between spirit worship and the adoration of the higher divinities.

Fear is a primordial affection of the human mind; and the continual terror which haunts savage men, as it does wild animals, and which is at the bottom of all superstition, seems to have been originally little more than the instinctive fright at strange sounds and sights that we can still see in domestic animals. We can judge how strong this terror must have been by noticing how long it has lasted. Just as the shying of a horse at a bush is the survival of the ancestral instinct that made his far-off progenitors shun anything strange and therefore dangerous, so, I think, the unreasoning horror that is apt to come over people at the image of a ghost, or even at a ghost story, is traceable backward to the times when our ancestors felt themselves to be surrounded by capricious or malignant beings. The fear of ghosts is the faint shadow still left on our imaginations by the universal belief of primitive folk that they were haunted by the spirits of the dead.

Now the essential characteristic of ghosts is given better by the French word than by the English—it is a *Revenant*, one that returns. And if I were asked to make a conjecture why this notion of the return or reappearance of a dead man's spirit is so widespread, I should reply by pointing to the one fundamental fact, the first and most formidable law—that comes home to all men and partly I suspect to some of the higher animals—the endless succession in Nature of Birth, Death, and Revival. I do not think it possible to overrate the deep impression that must be engraved on the minds of the early races of mankind by the continual perishing and reproduction of all animate things. To man in his wild state the same life appears to stir in everything, in running water, in a tree, and in a creature; it ends and disappears in everything at times, but it reappears again constantly, in shape, movement and outward character so similar as to seem identical; conveying the inference that something has gone and come again; there is nothing around a savage to suggest that the animating principle of vitality suffers more than suspension or displacement. The analogy of Nature affords him no presumption that death means extinction, while his imagination supplies him with constant evidence to the contrary.

But however this may be, one thing seems

sure, whatever may be the reason of it, that although the fact that all men die rests upon the most direct, conclusive, and unquestionable evidence, constantly renewed, yet no race of men ever seems to have accepted death as the certain end of the dead man's personality. Among primitive folk the presumption seems to have been exactly the reverse; they are all convinced that his soul has only gone elsewhere; they do not regard life as extinguished; they look for signs and tokens of it somewhere else; and they are incessantly haunted, asleep or awake, with the apparitions of familiar forms or hints of a familiar presence. This incapacity or desperate refusal to acquiesce in the finality of death powerfully affects all the primitive races of India; and it is my opinion that the notion of the survival, reappearance, and transmission of the soul or spirit runs like a spinal cord through the whole connected series of the beliefs that are comprised in Hinduism. It pervades, I think, all classes of Indian society; it is the chief motive of ritual, it explains the origin of many divinities, and it underlies some of the cardinal doctrines of high Brahmanic ortho-doxy. The notion is seen very plainly in the least advanced societies. The Khasia Hills, for example, are peopled by a very simple folk, whom until lately the propagation of Brahmanism had scarcely reached. In those hills, when a man dies far from home, his friends tie threads across the streams near his village, in order to provide the spirit with a bridge on his return journey; and I mention this particularly because the custom may throw some light on the well-known inability of Scottish elves and sprites to cross running water[1]. Among the Khasias also, when a man dies abroad, a cock is killed that the bird may wake the ghost early each day on his travel homeward; and as far as I could make out the indigenous religion consists almost wholly of the worship of the spirits of the dead.

[1] "If you can interpose a brook between you and witches, spectres, or even fiends, you are in perfect safety." Note to Scott's *Lay of the Last Minstrel.*

Now the beliefs of the Khasia folk are merely a sample of the ideas universally prevalent, among the aborigines of India, regarding the returning spirit. If again we go among the general settled population of Hindus, we find the same feelings persistent among them. The lament at a Hindu funeral says, "That which has spoken has gone —the Spirit has departed"—and at the same time there runs through their obsequies the notion that the wandering soul of the dead person must be provided with a new refuge, must be harboured, and comforted. As bodily death is a giving up of the ghost, he must be provided with a fresh tenement, or at least with some temporary accommodation ; and here comes in the very general custom among certain classes of Hindus, after a cremation, of picking up at the funeral pyre some small object in which the soul is supposed, by a fiction, to have taken refuge after the body has been burnt, and of carrying it back to the dead man's house.

You will observe that the belief in survival

involves the necessity of giving the homeless spirit some local habitation; he must take up his abode in something animate or inanimate, in a tree, an animal, or perhaps in queer look-ing stocks and stones. He is thus likely to be haunting places in some shadowy or sub-stantial form; he may be helping his friends and plaguing his enemies; his presence can be discovered by the breaking out of a disease, by an odd accident, or by the strange behaviour of an animal. One remarkable case is worth mentioning to an English audience. Some fifty years ago a very high English official died in a fortress, at a place that is one of the centres of Brahmanic orthodoxy; and at the moment when the news of his death reached the Sepoy guard at the main gate, a black cat rushed out of it. The guard presented arms to the cat as a salute to the flying spirit of the powerful Englishman; and the coincidence took so firm a hold of the locality that up to a few years ago neither exhortation nor orders could prevent a Hindu sentry at that gate from presenting arms to any cat that passed out of the fort at night.

My conjecture is that a great part of what is called Animism—the tendency to discover human life and agency in all moving things, whether waving trees or wandering beasts—begins with this ingrained conviction that some new form or habitation must be provided for the spirits of dead men. I do not pretend that in India the whole worship of trees and animals can be traced to this habit of the mind, but I believe that the widespread idea of possession by spirits or demons, particularly the very common notion that the soul of a wicked or miserable man is inside a wild beast, does come largely from the imaginary necessity of finding lodging and employment for ghosts.

Nothing indeed is more common in India than the belief that the spirits of dead men have passed into certain animals, and I could give some curious instances of the manner in which this passage of the spirit through an animal shape affects the subsequent developement of a deity, who often retains in his attributes, symbols, and mythology, the recollection of this earlier stage of his metamorphosis. But this is a side line of my main subject, and anticipates a later stage of it. I can only say here that in India the worship of animals becomes crossed and intertwined at a very early stage with the worship of spirits, in a manner very difficult to unravel ; that there is good evidence that as the ghost developed into a god, he retained some characteristic of the animal whom he may have at one time inhabited, which animal often became in a later stage one of the god's temporary embodiments. A serpent, for example, is unquestionably dreaded, and therefore worshipped, as a dangerous and mysterious beast ; and for that very reason he may be also treated as the embodiment of a malignant and subtle spirit recently passed away from among men. Later on the sacred snake is regarded as the shape into which some sage or semi-divine person has become transformed. And ultimately it becomes the emblem or allegorical symbol of a great god. I repeat, that at the bottom of all these imaginary changes lies the belief in survival, the notion that death is transmigration, and that man is encompassed by the restless and roving spirits of the dead, who have human wants and affections, and superhuman powers. All these fancies appear to me to become grouped and interlaced in the word superstition—a word that may have originally meant something like survival—and out of this atmosphere of ghostly terrors, griefs, and wonder the rudimentary deities seem to me to be continually issuing.

It is certain that in India one can distinctly follow the evolution of the ghosts of men whose life or death has been notorious, into gods. Wherever in India the beliefs can still be found in an elementary or indigenous state, wherever they appear to have grown up spontaneously, some of the principal deities can be identified with the spirits of departed humanity. When I lived for some years in a province of Central India that had been very little touched by external influences, I had many opportunities of personally verifying this fact. In the outlying districts one could find everywhere the worship of the spirits of men who had been distinguished for valour, wisdom, piety, or misfortune, for a notable life or a tragic death. Their Manes were propitiated; and if their power to harm or to help increased, their tombs might become shrines or temples; and the offerings to the dead might develope into sacrifices. The report that a god has lived on earth as a man, the fact that he has been perfectly well known in the neighbourhood, are no prejudice whatever to his subsequent dignity; though as his wonderworking reputation rises his earthly history becomes usually more dim and mystical; the legend comes in to disguise his mortal origin, and he veils himself more and more under divine attributes. If we look steadily at these processes, visible in the clear daylight of the present time, they may well seem to reflect, as in a mirror, the fables and mythologies of the antique world, and to throw a ray of light on their origin; while the reality of the thing is brought home to us by the fact that the spirits of more than one Englishman, and of one Englishwoman, are now worshipped in India. General Nicholson, who was killed in the storming of Delhi, had a sect of worshippers; and in South India they adore the spirit of Captain Pole, who was mortally wounded and died in a forest; the people dug his grave, built his shrine, and employed a local priest to devise a form of worship that was certainly going on within the last few years.

But the authentic transformation of the disembodied spirit into a superhuman being is contested by no one; the difficulty is only to disentangle the ghost, the divine ancestor, and the incipient deity with his attributes or special powers. They seem to be often blended, and their earthly and unearthly characters remain for a certain time interfused. We had last year a census of all India; and I noticed in an Indian newspaper of March last that one Hindu house-holder filled up his schedule by returning, as Head of the Family, his household deity, whose profession he described as subsistence on an endowment, while the question whether the divine personage was or was not literate was somewhat indirectly answered by entering him as Omniscient. At a later stage, when the divinity is once clearly established, his special attributes or department may be determined by an accident. We may take, as an example, the history of Hurdeo Lala who was, not very long ago, poisoned in Central India by his brother through jealousy. This was a sensational murder, not unlike that of Hamlet's father; and whereas in England he might have been commemorated by a tragic drama, a mournful ballad, or by a figure in a wax-work exhibition, in India temples were erected to him. Some time afterward, when the cholera broke out suddenly and fiercely in a camp that was pitched close to his shrine, it was

ascribed by public opinion to the displeasure of
his injured ghost, who was thus credited with
the power of letting loose epidemics ; so Hurdeo
Lala became the special god of cholera in that
region.   It is in this manner that dim shapes
and mere superstitious dread gradually give
place to the distinct image and definite attributes
of divinity.

Thus it seems to me, if I may here briefly
recapitulate, that everywhere in India the natural
propensity to adore curious, terrible, or beneficent
things has become crossed and mixed up with
the habit of detecting human spirits everywhere.
This leads to the deification of humanity; which
is throughout so much the strongest element in
the shaping of superstitious imagery that it
gradually absorbs all other elements.   And thus
the detection of divine power or purpose in plants
and animals, in stocks and stones, in plagues and
diseases, has a tendency to coalesce and harden
into the worship of some glorified man, who may
have the place as his sanctuary, the plant or

animal as his embodiment, or the plague as his attribute. The adoration is paid both to the object, and to the spirit that has become accidentally connected with the object, and the two lines of worship take human shape eventually.

It is true that the deification of notables does not go on in India in so regular and recognized a fashion as in China, where the gods and their ritual are under State patronage and authority, and where promotions from the lower to the higher grades of the Pantheon are often announced in the Official Gazette. In India Religion has always been, as I have said, independent of State supervision, and is only imperfectly controlled by the priesthood. The minor Indian spirit is left to rise by his own merit and by popular suffrage; the foreign governments that have so long ruled in India are either hostile or indifferent—and in these latter days the gradual spread of wider knowledge of the outer world, the general stir and movement of civilized and peaceful life, the spread of education, are undermining the whole fabric of these beliefs, and driving them into obscure corners. In the course of one or two generations they will probably dwindle down to the condition of paganism or heathenism ; they will be regarded as the quaint old-fashioned superstitions of the wolds or the remote rural districts ; and thus the embryonic stages of the generation of gods will gradually disappear. The origin of the divine species, the descent of the deities from man, may then come to be vigorously disputed by scholars and antiquarians; the saints and heroes will become fabulous and manifestly unreal, and their true evolution will be explained philologically, or demonstrated by the science of comparative mythology.

At present, however, the deification of ghosts can be unquestionably established by the collection of plentiful evidence in India. Of course I do not pretend that it covers the whole ground, or that it is more than one of the sources which have produced the confused multitude of deities that are worshipped there. And I am well aware that the genealogy of deities has been traced back to ancestral and spirit worship in various countries. Nevertheless we have never before been able to take such a comprehensive survey of the actual process; and the value of observations taken in India is that it gives us not only the earliest but the latest stages of deification, and shews us the connected series. We have at the bottom the universal worship of spirits partly ancestral and commemorative, in part propitiatory; we see them gradually transmuted into household gods, local deities, and divinities of special forms, attributes, and departments; while at the top we have the full-blown adoration of the lofty Brahmanic deities who preside over the operations of nature and the strongest passions of mankind.

The verification of such an important phase in the Natural History of polytheism seems to me not the least curious result of that remarkable contact and contrast between ancient and modern ideas and institutions, that is represented by the English in India. To us, whom political circumstances have brought more closely than any other modern nation into relation with archaic beliefs, it is of particular interest that we should find in India a strong corroboration of the theory that was adopted, from a point of view different yet not altogether dissimilar, by those who stood face to face with the decaying polytheism of the Roman empire. It was positively affirmed by the Christian Fathers and apologists that the gods of classic paganism were deified men. Tertullian challenges the heathen to deny it; and Augustine vehemently asserts it. "For with such blindness," he says, "do impious men, as it were, stumble over mountains, and will not see the things which strike their own eyes, that they do not attend to the fact that in all the literature of the Pagans there are not found any, or scarcely any, gods who have not been men to whom when dead divine honours were paid[1]."

You will remember that I began by throwing out the conjecture that the original bent or form of Natural Religion had been moulded upon the deep impression stamped on primitive minds by the perpetual death and reappearance, or re-suscitation, of animate things. And I argued that the incessant presence of this visible opera-tion, aided by the natural feelings of terror and regret, had generated in the imagination of the earliest races their intense conviction that the death of man is only the transmigration of his soul, that he only suffers a change of shape or abode. I suggested that this had contributed to produce spirit worship generally, and had led to the adoration of the more illustrious spirits, who were invested with superior powers, and became gods. Where now, in the upper grades of Hin-duism, may we observe the full growth and maturity of these primordial ideas? We see

[1] *De Civitate Dei.*

them, I think, magnified and reproduced upon a grand and imposing scale, in the supreme divinities of Hindu theology, in Vishnu and Siva; for Brahma, the creative energy, is too remote and abstract an influence for popular worship. Siva represents what I have taken to be the earliest and universal impression of Nature upon men— the impression of endless and pitiless change. He is the destroyer and rebuilder of various forms of life; he has charge of the whole circle of animated creation, the incessant round of birth and death in which all nature eternally revolves. His attributes are indicated by symbols emblematic of death and of man's desire; he presides over the ebb and flow of sentient existence. In Siva we have the condensation of the two primordial agencies, the striving to live and the forces that kill; and thus, philosophically speaking, we see in this great divinity a comprehensive transfiguration of that idea which, as I repeat, I hold to be the root of Natural Religion. He exhibits by images, emblems, and allegorical carvings the whole course and revolution of Nature, the inexorable law of the alternate triumph of life and death— Mors Janua Vitae—the unending circle of indestructible animation.

Vishnu, on the other hand, impersonates the higher evolution; the upward tendency of the human spirit. He represents several great and far-reaching religious ideas. In the increasing flux and change of all things he is their Preserver; and although he is one of the highest gods he has constantly revisited the earth either in animal or in human shape. What are the modes and ascending flights by which the spirits, who have been deified for their valour, sanctity, or beneficence, are brought into relation with this supreme conception of divinity? They rise by the medium of the Avatárs, the descents or reappearances of Vishnu, who personifies the doctrine of successive divine embodiments, which is one of the most important in Hinduism. Most of the famous saints, heroes, and demigods of poetry and romance, with many of the superior divinities, are recognized as having been the sensible manifestations of Vishnu; their bodies were only the mortal vesture that he assumed for the purpose of interposing decisively at some great emergency, or whenever he condescended to become again an actor in the world's drama. It must be clearly understood that this theory of the divine embodiment is one of the most essential and effective doctrines of Hinduism; it links together and explains the various phases of the religion, connecting the lower with the higher ideas, and providing them with a common ground or method of reconciliation. It serves to shew, for instance, that the sacred animal of a wild tribe is merely the great Brahmanic deity in disguise, or it may prove that the worshippers of some obscure or local hero have been adoring Vishnu unawares. It thus accommodates and absorbs the lower deities; and while it draws them up to the sky and completes their apo-theosis, it also brings the higher gods constantly down again from heaven to take part in human affairs. We thus find running through all Hinduism, first the belief in the migration of spirits when divorced from the body, next their deification, and latterly their identification with the supreme abstract divinities. But these supreme divinities reappear again in various earthly forms; so that there is a continual passage to and fro between men and gods, gods and men. And thus we have the electric current of all-pervading divine energy completing its circle through diverse forms, until we reach the conception of all Nature being possessed by the divinity.

We are now on the limit of that which I take to be the intellectual climax of the evolution of Natural Religion—I mean the doctrine of Pantheism. The adoration of innumerable spirits becomes gradually collected into the main channels and runs into the anthropomorphic moulds of the higher polytheism, which again is still further condensed into the recognition of the Brahmanic Trinity under multitudinous

shapes, signs, and attributes. And as all rivers
end in the sea, so every sign, symbol, figure, or
active energy of divinity, is ultimately regarded
as the outward expression of that single universal
divine potency, which is everywhere immanent
in the world, which in fact *is* the World.

I must guard myself from being understood
to hold that the deification of humanity accounts
for all Hinduism ; for in India every visible
presentation of force, everything that can harm
or help mankind, is worshipped ; at first instinc-
tively and directly, latterly as the token of
divinity working behind the phenomenal veil.
We have of course to take into account the
direct adoration paid to the mountains and
rivers, to the Sun and the Moon, to the Sky and
Winds, and to such abstract personifications as
the goddess Fortune. And into the allegorical
and mythological branch of this vast subject I
cannot here enter.

It is now time for me to turn to another side
of Hinduism, to its Ritual, which is in its early

stages a vast method of propitiation, and latterly a lofty kind of ceremonial liturgy. My view is that just as the higher polytheism is connected by descent with the aboriginal veneration of dis-embodied spirits, so likewise much of the ritual can be followed back, in India, to primitive obse-quies, to methods for laying the ghost, for feeding, comforting, and conciliating him. Many years ago, on my road home to England, I travelled straight from the depths of Central India to Paris, and on the Boulevards I came suddenly to a stand before a fashionable mourning warehouse, which had in large letters on the plate glass the motto *Le deuil c'est un culte*—Mourning is Wor-ship. As this was precisely the conclusion that had been suggested to me a month earlier, by the sight of the funeral rites of the Bheels, a wild folk in the jungles, I was startled by finding it pro-claimed in Paris as an advertisement of crape and black silk. And I began to consider whether this might not be the attenuated survival of a remote but once universal idea. For the ceremonies, the

honours and attentions paid to the dead, among
primitive societies in India, seemed to me in-
tended to please and provide for the ghost ; and
some trace of this purpose may be discerned in
almost every stage or gradation of funeral services
among Hindus, from the lowest to the highest,
from the offerings made to the dead and the
wailing prayers of the rude tribes, up to the
formal oblations prescribed by the Brahmanic
High Church. You may have heard, for example,
that the right to inherit property is by Hindu
law co-extensive with the duty of making certain
periodical offerings to the ancestral spirits.

I agree, therefore, that mourning in its original meaning partook largely of the nature of
worship. I think the prayers were not for the
dead man but addressed to him, that the funeral
service was usually an offer or an attempt to do
him service. And I find reason to believe that
whenever a spirit became gradually translated to
some higher degree of divinity, the earlier propitiation of the wandering ghost passed into a

form of worship, that the offerings at the grave
or shrine became sacrifices in the temple. Now
I submit to you the general remark that in no
existing religious system does sacrifice play such
an important part, occupy such high ground, as
in Hinduism. In the ancient world it may be
said to have been almost an universal practice,
the most essential of all religious observances.
In the modern world it has almost entirely
disappeared. It lingers in Mahomedanism as a
figurative or commemorative act; in Buddhism
the offerings are not propitiatory; they are pious
gifts reverentially presented, chiefly as alms to
the priesthood. But in India we can still see
with our eyes the performance of sacrifices in
almost every stage or step of an ascending scale;
there is every variety of offering; the wild tribes
slaughter buffaloes to the goddess Devi; the
altars of Siva, in the heart of Calcutta, stream
with the blood of goats; and although human
sacrifice and self-sacrifice by suicide have now
been everywhere suppressed, yet traditional

remains of these customs still circulate in the outlying parts of the country. The Brahmans do their best to discourage and refine these savage rites, but as in the matter of the ruder gods so in regard to their ritual, the priesthood has never been strong enough to purify and regulate all the discordant usages of a most diversified society. It has thus come to pass that some very rough and barbarous rites are practised side by side with the pure and lofty ceremonial of the Vedic devotions. The idol may be the god itself, may be the consecrated image in which the deity is present, or may be merely the token or point for prayer and meditation; and according to the votary's conception of the god so is the intention and meaning of the sacrifice. The lowest conception seems to be that of providing food or service for the ghost, the highest is of a sin offering, or mysterious atonement.

Human sacrifice is one of the earliest forms of the rite. How did it first begin? Some very ingenious and intricate explanations of its origin

have recently been suggested; I myself doubt
whether we can go back with any certainty
beyond the motive of pleasing or paying due
honour to the ghost of some powerful personage.
Perhaps the earliest notion to be found now
authentically existing, not in India, but upon
the Indian borderland, is that of dispatching
slaves or companions to accompany a dead chief
on his journey into the next world—that is, into
his new state of existence or abode. The tribes
of our North-East frontier still make occasional
raids upon the villages of the plain for the
purpose of capturing Bengalees, whom they slay
at the funeral of a chief in order to provide him
with a retinue. In the case of prisoners taken
in war there may also be the desire of finding
a plausible, what we might call a sanctimonious,
pretext for getting rid of them by slaying them
on the altar; for nothing is more common than
to find a sacred duty used to veil some motive
of direct human interest or utility. However
this may be, there is strong evidence connect-

ing human sacrifice in India with funeral obsequies; and the view which I venture to put before you is that by the same process of development which converted the spirit into a deity, the slaying of slaves and captives to attend the departing ghost becomes the offering up of victims to powerful gods. There is no doubt whatever that human sacrifice has been held, is held, in India as elsewhere, to be a sovereign remedy for appeasing the wrath of the gods. Most of us have heard of the Meriah sacrifices among the Khonds, who periodically slaughtered human victims. There is moreover a well-authenticated case of an English official finding a victim tied up before a shrine during a sharp epidemic of cholera; and there was another mysterious incident not very long ago at a temple in that city which is chiefly given up to the worship of the great god Siva. I may mention, also, that certain unaccountable and apparently motiveless murders, very like those which frightened East London last year, have occasionally been committed ; and were probably due to the accomplishment of a vow.

But systematic human sacrifice, except among a few savage tribes, must have disappeared long ago from India. Such traditions of the custom as remain, point to the idea of resorting to it only on some great emergency or mysterious difficulty indicating divine displeasure. There is one world-wide and inveterate superstition belonging to the sacrificial class, of which we have many vestiges in India—it is the belief that a building can be made strong, can be prevented from falling, by burying alive some one, usually a child, under its foundations.

Grimm, in his *Teutonic Mythology*, gives stories shewing the prevalence of this custom in North Europe before the Teutonic tribes were Christianized. And the tradition still over-shadows the imagination of primitive folk in India. I recollect that when one of the piers of a railway bridge was washed away by a flood in Central India, there was a panic among the

tribes of the neighbouring hills, who were possessed by the rumour that one of them was to
be seized and buried in the basement when the
pier should be rebuilt. The ghost of such a
victim becomes naturally deified. On the bas-
tion of many of the forts in that country is a sort
of mimic grave or shrine, sacred to a dead man
who is said to have been sacrificed long ago to
keep up the wall of a fortress, and who has now
become the tutelary spirit of bastions. But the
Moghul emperor, Shah Jehan, was humane
enough to bury goats instead of men under the
walls of his fortified palace; and there has probably been a steady transition to milder forms
of consecration. We still, in England, bury
something, though only a few coins, under a
foundation-stone; and without pretending to
connect this formula with any ritualistic origin,
I may say that theories have been strung together on quite as far-fetched and as fanciful
lines of association.

But sacrifice may also be voluntary, upon

public or private grounds; and religious suicide has always had much vogue in India. There is a story of the commander of an army, who turned the adverse tide of battle by causing himself to be beheaded in front of his troops as a sacrifice to the gods. And though in military history I have discovered no other instance of a general who won an action by losing his head at a critical moment, yet the legend illustrates the persistence of the central idea that great emergencies demand supreme propitiatory acts. I admit, however, that to the sceptical mind, which discerns under every observance the germ of utilitarian motive, the story may present itself as no more than a pious invention to sanctify the sudden violent removal of an incapable or unlucky leader.

Let me now refer to the highest form of human self-sacrifice, the latest to disappear in some parts of India. I mean the custom of Suttee. In the burning of Hindu widows on the funeral pyre of their husbands, we may perceive two or three motives intertwined; we have, first, the primordial idea of sending a wife to accompany her husband into the next world, secondly the much later doctrine, that for a widow to die in this manner with her husband is an act of the purest and noblest devotion, and lastly comes in the irrepressible utilitarian motive of liberating a great man's estate from the very serious burden of dowry for several widows. Some years ago a Hindu nobleman, with whom I was acquainted, had to support twelve of his father's widows; and those who have seen in Rajputana, on the marble tombs or cenotaphs of the chiefs, a long row of the figures of the wives and slave girls who were burnt with some great Rajah three or four generations back, might easily appreciate the danger to which the temptation of putting away defenceless women might expose widows in the dark ages of India.

These things were done, however, as Macbeth says, in the olden time, "ere human statute purged the gentle weal"—that is, before Governments were strong enough to support the higher morality of India in suppressing them. The savage forms of sacrifice are now extinct, but the later and milder varieties of immolation and offering exist in great abundance, far greater, as I have said, than in any other civilized country. The Ritual is the outward and visible sign of natural piety ; for piety, as we are told in a Socratic dialogue[1], is a sort of science of praying and sacrificing, of asking and giving; it is there explained as the art which gods and men have of doing business with each other. This definition, given at Athens more than 2000 years ago, exactly fits in with the apparent object of the ritual of Indian polytheism. And indeed the whole aspect of polytheistic religion in India is to me that of an open market or bazaar, in which these dealings are carried on under every kind of ensign, by every kind of device and method of intercourse, among an infinite number of establishments and correspondents.

[1] Euthyphro.

For the characteristics of Natural Religion, the conditions of its existence as we see it in India, are complete liberty and material tolerance; there is no monopoly either of divine powers or even of sacerdotal privilege; since the Brahmans, though a most exclusive caste, are not an exclusive priesthood. No deity is invested with a supreme prerogative; no teacher proclaims himself the sole proprietor of the secret of the divine will; the army of the gods is not a fixed establishment; nor has the State ever asserted authority over the public worship. In India the British Government is more absolutely disconnected with religion than in any other part of Her Majesty's dominions; it interposes only when barbarous customs fall within the range of the ordinary penal code; and in fact the whole art and practice of Hinduism still lies open, as it has always done, to the changing influences of social and political environment.

It is this unrestrained indulgence of the religious propensities, this immemorial immunity

from authoritative limitation, that has made
India so important a field of study, especially
for those who desire to understand the ancient
polytheisms. For in the gradual transforma-
tions of the divine figures is seen the free and
natural working of the radical ideas that seem
to have inspired the earliest forms of superstition
everywhere, and to have determined their subsequent expansion. As with the gods, so with
their ritual; one may see in India the stages
and transitions; one may fancy that their pedi-
gree can be identified, may find corroboration of
the hypothesis that most of these customs and
practices can be traced to a few primary sources.

What does Hobbes, in the *Leviathan*, call
the Natural Seed of Religion? "And in these
Foure Things," (he says), "Opinion of Ghosts,
Ignorance of Second Causes, Devotion toward
what men fear, and Taking of Things casual for
Prognostiques, consisteth the Natural Seed of
Religion, which by reason of the different
Fancies, Judgments, and Passions of severall

men, hath grown up into ceremonies so different that those which are used by one man are for the most part ridiculous to another."

These words, quaint and stiff as they are, appear to me to cover most of the ground out of which polytheism in India has grown up, and, what is more, can be still seen growing. I do not mean that the process of transformation is always upward—I think that the strong tendency of beliefs and customs to improve is counteracted by another tendency toward degradation. I could give examples to shew that a pure and exalted religious conception very often suffers decay and corruption, that spiritualism relapses into idolatry. But this is because the Upper Hinduism has never been organized authoritatively, has never acquired the concentrated and sustained leverage that enables a powerful Church to lift the lower beliefs permanently up to the higher level. In Europe and Western Asia the lesser worships and loose invertebrate beliefs have been systematically extirpated by Christianity and Islam, whereby the whole religious landscape has been entirely altered. The establishment of Churches and uncompromising Creeds, with the enormous support given to them for centuries by autocratic and orthodox Governments, has laid out the ground of Religion like a stately and well ordered domain. Even under the Roman empire Religion was largely the concern of the State, the city, or the nation; and in modern Europe the sense of uniformity, discipline, and symmetry in matters of faith and worship, has become deeply impressed on our minds by long habit and the force of law. Popular Hinduism, on the contrary, is left to multitudinous confusion; for it defies limitation, and it is obviously useless to stamp as pure and genuine any particular image or doctrine of divinity, if a great many others may issue and pass current simultaneously. And this state of things seems likely, to judge from the past history of religions, to continue so long as

Hinduism remains without any central influence or superior control, but goes on reproducing itself and spreading from the natural seed. In short, the whole panorama of religious ideas and practices, in polytheistic India, may be compared to the entangled confusion of a primeval forest, where one sees trees of all kinds, ages, and sizes interlacing and contending with each other; some falling into decay, others shooting up vigorously and overtopping the crowd—while the glimpse of blue sky above the tree tops may symbolize the illimitable transcendental ideas above and apart from the earthborn conceptions.

For it must always be remembered that the dominant idea of intellectual Hinduism, the belief which overhangs all this jungle of superstitions, is the Unity of the Spirit under a plurality of forms. Every religion must be in accord with the common experiences and needs of the people; but if it is to keep its hold on the higher minds it must also rest somewhere upon a philosophic theory; and Pantheism is the

Philosophy of Natural Religion. The identity of all divine energies underlying this incessant stir and semblance of life in the world is soon recognized by reflective minds; the highest god as well as the lowest creature is a mere vessel of the Invisible Power; the god is only a peculiar and extraordinary manifestation of that power; the mysterious allegorical Trinity, Brahma, Vishnu, Siva, at the summit of Hinduism suggests and personifies its regular unchanging operation. It is of little use for those who attack Hinduism to insist that the mythology is a romance, or a disease of language; that the divinities are phantasms, that the idols are merely carved stones or cunning casts of clay. The higher Brahmans would probably agree that the popular polytheism is not much more than a pious mystery play exhibiting under various masks and costumes the marvellous drama of Nature, in which the divine power is immanent, and with which it is identical. They would say that the deities themselves are but signs and shadows of the Incomprehensible. This Pantheism is not an abstruse theologic doctrine; it is ingrained in the minds of all thoughtful persons; the inner meaning lies everywhere close below the outward worship, and it comes out at the first serious question. Queer idols and grotesque rites are to be seen everywhere in India, yet if any one were to challenge the priest or the worshipper to justify or explain them, he might very possibly receive an answer that would startle him by its subtlety, and by the momentary disclosure of some profound meaning underlying the irrational and superficial observance. And so Pantheism may be regarded as the final stage in the fusion and combination of the multitude of forms and conceptions bred out of vagrant superstitions; it does not stamp out or abolish them; it hardly cares to improve them; it explains and finds room for them all. To borrow a metaphor from *In Memoriam,* Pantheism is the Godless Deep into which the ever-breaking shore of primitive beliefs is constantly tumbling; it is the last stage of Nature Worship.

But forms and ceremonies, prayer and sacrifice, are useful only within the limits of this visible world, which is for gods as well as for men the sphere of action and concern. The highest devotion of Hinduism has for its object spiritual knowledge, the rescue of the soul from the ocean of illusory ephemeral existence; and this liberation is attained by 'the soul's passage through the vicissitudes of innumerable lives. Even here it is possible, I believe, to discern the remote influence of the persistent analogy from Nature ; for there is no extravagance in supposing that the great Hindu dogma of the transmigration of souls still prolongs metaphysically the rule of change and transition by which the whole apparent universe is, to the Indian, so manifestly governed. The material conception of the homeless, wandering ghost, whom death is constantly dislodging, who may become a god, and again become a man, reappears in the moral doctrine of the laborious travel of the soul through many forms, through a labyrinth of painful and purifying existences; it is the promulgation of Natural law in the Spiritual world. According to this doctrine every human being has suffered a long series of births and dissolutions, his present condition being the necessary consequence of his precedent doings or experiences. And the range of his diverse existences stretches from a vegetable to a divinity; for gods also are subject to the law which governs the world of sensation. The same soul that moved in the flower may re-appear in the god; and we can here perceive that this doctrine mysteriously points to or shadows out the inner meaning of the con-nexion or common basis that underlies and holds together the lower and higher forms of external worship.

Every successive death does indeed interrupt consciousness; but so does sleep; and as in the visible world our birth is but a sleep and a forgetting, while we nevertheless inherit the

qualities, good or bad, of our progenitors ; so
between each stage of its journey the soul loses
all remembrance of the past, yet its next life is
influenced by the merits or demerits accumu-
lated in previous states. I venture to suggest
that the upward striving of Nature through the
modifications of forms and species is reflected,
as in a glass, darkly, by this vision of spiritual
evolution that gradually liberates the soul from
the bondage of conscious existence, that purges
it from the periodical returns of life's fitful fever,
and brings it to final release by absorption into
the one Essence. Then at last it is seen that
all the changes of mortal life are merely illusions
of the Sense; that, as Lady Macbeth has said,
the sleeping and the dead are but as pictures ;
and that this manifold working of Nature is but
a kind of embroidery on the Curtain which
hangs before the illumination of true spiritual
knowledge.

" And as," says one of their text-books, " by
spreading out a picture, all its figures are ren-

dered plainly visible, so the apparent existence of the world is due to Máya—that is to say Illusion. With the destruction of this Illusion by knowledge phenomena are reduced to Unreality—just as the figures in the picture disappear when the canvas is rolled up."

I have thus endeavoured to give some general outline and measure of the vast difference in religious ideas and observances that separates the lower from the higher beliefs in India. It is the difference between the primitive belief in the survival and constant re-embodiment of the human ghost, and the philosophical notion of the soul's passage through a cycle of existences until it is absorbed into Spiritual Being. It is the difference between the superstition that every moving thing or wandering animal is possessed by a peculiar spirit, and the discovery that all nature is imbued by one divine energy. From the feeling that a god is phenomenally everywhere, the train of thought advances to the conviction that God is phenomenally nowhere, to the idealism that regards the whole world as a subjective creation of one's own illusive fancy. Although these differences are extreme, and cover from point to point the whole range of natural theology, yet they are not treated in Hinduism as mutually hostile or inconsistent; the higher ideas and observances tolerate, adopt, and interpret the lower; the worshipper at an ordinary temple, a man who adores a shapeless image, may, probably does, hold the highest Unitarian doctrines. His mind finds no difficulty in reconciling shifting multiformity at the base of his religion, with changeless Unity at the summit. No one, certainly not I, can pretend to give a clear demonstration of the whole line of connexion, or to follow the processes of imagination and thought which lead from the belief in millions of gods to the recognition of one Universal Spirit, or to the final conclusion that He is Unknowable. I can only say that the impression produced upon myself, after long personal observation of Religion in India, is that the whole of this marvellous structure comes by what, for want of a better term, I must call Natural Growth.

www.ingramcontent.com/pod-product-compliance
Ingram Content Group UK Ltd.
Pitfield, Milton Keynes, MK11 3LW, UK
UKHW020448010325
455719UK00015B/471